MEDITATION 24

BEST 24 MEDITATION TECHNIQUES - MTTC-IYO

PDT. MANAS RAJRISHI

Made with ♥ on the Notion Press Platform
www.notionpress.com

Om Namo Gurubhyo Gurupadukabhyon.

Namah parebhyah parapadukabhyah ||

Acharya Siddheshwar Padukabhyon

Namostu Lakshmipati Padukabhyah ||1||

Salutations to all the Gurus, Salutations to the Padukas of all the Gurus. Salutations to the Gurus or Paragurus of Shri Gurudev Ji and their Padukas.

Salutations to the Padukas of Acharyas and masters of Siddha Vidyas. Salutations to Shri Gurupadukas again and again.

Ajna Timirandhasya Gyananjan Shalakaya.

Chakshurunmeelitam yen tasmai Shri Gurve Namah ||

Salute to the Guru who opened the eyes of people blinded by the darkness of ignorance with the light of knowledge.

Millions of salutations to the feet of Sri Sri Anandmurthy Ji.

|| ॐ ||

Contents

Contents

Foreword

My fortunate nature showed the worldly me the path of Yoga. Now I know why Gurusatta(Gurus Empire) was subtly supporting me on this path. It is said that it is not easy to change oneself, but those who change are one in a million. I don't consider myself one in a million, but perhaps this is what Gurusatta is trying to do. With the inspiration of Gurusatta, the feeling of love for nature, compassion, kindness and love got stronger within me. These feelings naturally started explaining the secret of meditation to me. Meditation was becoming a topic in the market, so it was necessary to write about it. I had been fond of writing for some time but as a result of inspiration from Gurusatta, this is my first book.

Meditation is considered the main subject of yoga practice. There are two types of practitioners who practice meditation, one is worldly and the other is ascetic. Coming to the path of meditation for a worldly person does not at all mean turning away from the world, rather it means understanding worldliness more deeply and systematically so that he starts beautifying the world like meditation. Whereas if a Sanyasi is a meditator then it is necessary to make his Sanyasi life meaningful along with the path of happiness. Meditation is not a commercial product but it is a mystery in which to become a practitioner one has to start from the unit. Nowadays people come to business centers after meditating, their mind remains calm for some time and then life remains as it was.

Meditation is a path which improves the standard of life. In fact, if you understand the secret of this meditation and become a seeker, then every aspect of your life will become excellent. There will be a miraculous improvement in deteriorated health soon, progress will be made in business, sweet harmony will be established in the family, you will be saved from accidents, sleep will be balanced, work will be done with full concentration, memory power of students will develop manifold.

Inspired by God, many unhappy people came and I got the opportunity to serve them. Till date, I have heard from every person who has come here that meditation has played the biggest role in making his life happy. In this book you will be able to know the truth and main methods of meditation along with special secrets of meditation.

We will learn about the nature of meditation. We have seen this not only in India but in many religions of the world. I also believe that no religion is untouched by meditation.

We have put together 24 types of meditation methods and divided them into two parts. First is internal meditation, second is external meditation. By dividing meditation in this way it became easier to understand the mystery of meditation.

॥ भू ॥

Preface

At present, I see that many yoga teachers, despite having obtained advanced degrees in yoga, remain untouched by the essence and methods of meditation. The business of Yoga is growing both in medical and educational form, in such a situation both become incomplete due to lack of mastery over the subject of meditation.

I have specially prepared this book for yoga students and yoga teachers. Depending on the different problems of life, the results of the treatment can be made easier by including the related meditation in all types of therapy. Also, this meditation will be very helpful for other readers to increase the balance in their normal life.

॥ भुवः ॥

Introduction Of Meditation

Definition Of Meditation

"Tatra Pratyayak Tanata Dhyanam" || Yogasutra-3/2

That is, wherever the mind is concentrated, the constant movement of the instincts is called meditation. Dharana means to bring or fix the mind at one place. But meditation means wherever the mind is fixed, the constant movement of the instinct in it is meditation. Staying awake in it is meditation.

"Meditation is awakening from within" – Osho

"The way to attain God by making the body a laboratory is meditation." - Sant Rajendra Singh Ji, Sant Kripal Spiritual Mission

"Meditation means opposing restlessness, or reducing restlessness." - Acharya Mahapragya

Types Of Meditation

Here meditation is basically divided into two parts –

1. Inner Meditation 2. External Meditation

1. Inner Meditation – The meditation in which we meditate on actions, energy, words and scenes within the body has been kept in the category of Antah Dhyana.

2. External Meditation - The meditation in which attention is focused on actions, words, energy and visuals outside the body has been kept in the category of external meditation.

Here there are two types of meditation and addition, from the basic category of internal and external.

3.Iinner outer Meditation and 4.Infinite Meditation

According to Gherand Samhita, there are three types of meditation -

Gross meditation (big meditation) (Sthool Dhyan)– some place like forest, garden etc.

2. Light meditation (eye meditation) (Jyotirmay Dhyan)- between the eyebrows.

3. Subtle Meditation (Small Meditation)(Sukshma Dhyan) – For those who have reached the pinnacle of Yoga.

According to Bhakti Sagar, there are four types of meditation –

Padastha meditation, 2. Pindastha meditation, 3. Rupastha meditation, 4. Rupateet meditation

Apart from this, Lord Buddha has discovered Vipassana meditation.

Elements of Meditation

According to the methods, meditation is done through the following activities.

1. Action Element – In meditation, when concentration is done on some action in the body or outside the body.

2.Fire Element – In meditation, when concentration is done on visible or invisible visuals outside or within.

3. Sky Element – In meditation when concentration is done on sound.

4.Smell Element – In meditation when concentration is done on natural fragrances.

5. Air Element – In meditation, when concentration is done on touch.

6.Mixed Elements – In meditation, when the mind concentrates on all the elements like sight, words, touch and smell along with action.

॥ स्वः॥

Inner Meditation

Inner Meditation means meditation within the body. If you do not have the practice of going into meditation directly, then you can do any of these activities for a while first. With these activities it will become easier to stabilize the mind.

1. Continuous rapid breathing for 10 minutes. Like Bhrastrika, Kapalbhati, rhythmic breathing, Anulom-Vilom etc.

2. Lick all parts of the body seven times (except inappropriate places).

3. Taking bath before meditation.

4. Laugh out loud.

5. To pray passionately.

6. After yogasanas.

CHAPTER ONE

Pranakarshna meditation (Life Attraction Meditation)

Pranakarshna is mentioned in the methods of pranayama, basically this pranakarshna pranayama is pranakarshna meditation. This meditation has a special effect on the life force, and also, Pranakarshna meditation is best for quickly curing any disease or ending pain in the body.

Method –

First of all sit in Shavasana, Siddhasana, Sukhasana, Vajrasana or Padmasana. Close your eyes and concentrate on breathing. Feel the effect of breathing internally as far as you can. When you start experiencing breathing completely, then do the process of breathing with Puraka, Antha Kumbhaka, Rechak and Bahya Kumbhaka. That is, slowly inhale completely, then hold the breath inside for some time, then slowly exhale and then hold it out for some time.

Next, concentrate your attention on the relaxation of the breath. That is, stabilize the mind after exhaling. For about 5 minutes, with the exhalation, make the main feeling that whenever the breath comes out, the inner impurity comes out, then one after the other make the feeling that the inner ego is coming out with the breath, the inner negativity. The inner powerlessness is coming out with the breath, the inner anger is coming out with the breath, the inner laziness is coming out with the breath, the inner greed is coming out with the breath, The sadness within is coming out with the breath, the ignorance within is coming out with the breath, the misfortune within is coming out with the breath, the sorrow within is coming out with the breath and the disease within is coming out with the breath. |

After doing the above meditation on Rechak for 5 minutes, focus on Purak for 5 minutes i.e. knowing within the breath. Make the main idea in the supplement that whenever the breath is entering inside, the energies of nature, cosmic energies and divine energies are going inside along with the breath. Then create expressions with complements one after the other – with the inhale the energies of the sun are going in, with the inhale positivity is going in, with the inhale the faith is going in, with the inhale the faith is going in, inhale With the breath going in, kindness is going in. With the breath going in, the knowledge energy is going in. With the breath going in, the love energy is going in. With the breath going in, fearlessness is going in. Auspicious energy is going inside.

Then, last of all, feel the joy and peace entering inside with the breath. In the end, experience the positive effects obtained after meditation and then come back to normal state by doing some movement in the fingers and toes. In this way, there is no need for Kumbhaka to spend much time meditating for 5 minutes on laxative and 5 minutes on puraka because the basic element of concentration is puraka and puraka. After this meditation is accomplished, meditation can be done on Antha Kumbhaka and Bahya Kumbhaka.

Puraka = Inhale, Rechak=Exhale, Antah Kumbhaka=Inhale then hold, Bahya Kumbhaka=Exhale then hold

॥ ततः॥

CHAPTER TWO

Bhrikuti Meditation (Rupastha Dhyana)

Sitting in any suitable posture, looking between the eyebrows is Bhrikuti meditation. If you are doing this meditation for the first time, then doing it for 3 minutes is enough. Later, if you increase the practice, it can be done for a longer time.

Benefits - This meditation has a special effect on concentration power. The inner knowledge blossoms. Rajyoga is attained. Many saints have also included Bhrikuti meditation among the main subjects of meditation.

Some common methods – I do not have the capacity to access the experiences of specific great men to tell the best method of this meditation. But I am describing the general method for worldly men.

First of all, close your eyes and sit in any suitable yoga asana, allow your body and mind to automatically calm down, then slowly try to concentrate your vision between the eyebrows. Once the vision is concentrated, understand the scene seen in the middle. First of all small particles of fire are visible. After doing this for several days, a light like the flame of a lamp becomes visible. Gradually, within a few days, garlands of stars, lightning, moon, sun, sky etc. become visible.

In this way, do normal activities for 3 to 5 minutes daily. Once you have practiced in this way, Chakrabeej Mantra meditation is described further and after understanding the method of Ajna Chakra, you can do it separately for 10-15 minutes.

॥ सः ॥

CHAPTER THREE

Chakra Meditation -Part 1

Kavach Meditation

This is a special armor before any chakra meditation, with this armor it becomes easier to meditate.

Armor (Kavach)Method - Sitting in any meditative posture, first concentrate the mind on the outer shell of the body i.e. the skin. Touch and heat are felt through the skin. Feel the touch of air and atmospheric heat on the skin. Again go to the second inner layer, that is, feel the muscles, feel the blood circulation between the muscles. Then further concentrate on the skeleton. Feel for some time that you are just a skeleton, then shrink from all the skeletons and concentrate only on the spine.

Go inside the spine again and feel the flow of Susumna Nadi minutely here. It will seem to you as if there is a cavernous passage in the middle of the spine in which the most powerful energy flows within.

Before the end of the meditation, one has to come back from the armor exactly the same way. That is, positive energies should come from Susumna to the spinal cord, then through the entire skeleton, through muscles to the skin and come back to normal state with positive experiences.

After experiencing this energy it will become easier to experience the chakras. In line with these chakras, a feeling of chakras will be felt at the front end of the body. The connection of the chakras with the spinal cord and spinal cord is like the connection of a tree with the soil and nutrients.

The 7 main chakras as they appear in the body are:

Muladhara Chakra – Root Chakra.

Swadhishthana Chakra – Sacral Chakra.
Manipura Chakra – Solar Plexus Chakra.
Anahata Chakra – Heart Chakra.
Vishuddha Chakra – Throat Chakra.

Ajna Chakra – Third Eye Chakra.
Sahastrara Chakra – Crown Chakra.

॥ वि:॥

CHAPTER FOUR

Chakra Meditation-Part-2

Chakranubhuti Meditation - Meditation to feel the Chakras

Mainly 7 types of chakras are described in yoga texts - 1. Muladhar, 2. Swadhisthana, 3. Manipura, 4. Anahat, 5. Vishuddhi, 6. Ajna and 7. Sahasrara. Knowing the location of these seven chakras and experiencing all the chakras one after the other starting from the Muladhara Chakra is Chakranubhuti meditation. This is the first method of meditating on the chakras.

Method –

First of all feel the Chakra from Muladhar Chakra. If there is no sensation, you can also pull the anus up slightly. After getting the sensation, concentrate your mind on one chakra for about 3 minutes, then come back to normal state and experience the Susumna Nadi, then understand the path of the Susumna Nadi and rise up in the same path, reach Swadhisthana i.e. in line with the navel and then experience the Chakra there. After about 3 minutes, come back to Susumna Nadi and experience the Chakra on the way to Manipur. In this way, experience the cycles one after the other. Do eyebrow meditation in Ajna Chakra and do the same practice on all other chakras.

Special - A meditative person can experience Chakra directly even without primary activities. But by doing the primary activities, along with chakra meditation, one also meditates on Susumna Nadi. Instead of meditating by reading or hearing about the Chakras from various places, it is better to meditate by experiencing the Chakras.

॥ तु: ॥

CHAPTER FIVE

Chakra Meditation-Part-3

Chakra Rotation Meditation

All the chakras rotate like the picture. In this meditation, by feeling the rotation of the chakras, rhythm increases in it. Giving rhythmic flow in the rotation is called chakra rotation meditation.

Method -

Sit in any meditative meditation, complete the primary kavacha in the above meditation, then feel the chakras through the sensation of Susumna Nadi and experience the rotation in them. First of all start from Muladhara Chakra. Feel the rotation of the chakra at the Muladhara Chakra. If you don't have any experience, concentrate completely there. After some time you will start feeling the rotation of the wheel. The correct direction of the chakra is clockwise, so check simultaneously whether the rotation is rhythmic in the right direction or not. When the investigation is complete, concentrate more deeply on the rotation of the chakra. Establish the mind within the circle of rotation. Move the mind with rotation. Listen to the musical flow of nature.

Move the mind in a rotating motion with the musical flow. After completing one cycle, do one cycle after another for about 3 minutes. Finally, come out of each shell, feeling the rhythmic rotation of each chakra.

॥ व: ॥

CHAPTER SIX

Chakra Meditation -Part-4

Chakra Beej Mantra Meditation

In the Yoga Sadhana of Chakras, the Beej Mantra action of Chakras is most important. The activities of Yogasadhana are devoid of Veda mantras, but the Beej Mantra is the Adi Mantra like the Veda mantras. Just as there are special methods for chanting other mantras, in the same way in yoga practice, it is necessary to understand the method for chanting the seed mantra of the chakras. Nowadays, hypocrites have created a market in the name of Chakras.

There are two parts of this activity, the first part is Saptachakra Sadhana, the second is Ekachakra Sadhana. While meditating on one chakra after another, do Beej mantra meditation on all the seven chakras. Ordinary devotees should first do normal activities for several consecutive days.

Method-

First sit in any meditative posture, close your eyes as per the aforesaid Chakra Kriya and complete the Dhyana Kavacha. After Kavach, when the mind gets concentrated till the Susumna Nadi, then take the mind to Muladhar. Connect the vital air with the chakra. Complement, feel the effect of breathing till the chakra. Feel that the breath is reaching the chakra. After Puraka, also experience Kumbhaka on the Chakra. At the time of Kumbhaka on the Chakra, visualize a "red lotus with four petals". As long as the Kumbhaka lasts, chant the Beej Mantra "Lam" repeatedly on the chakra with mental words, then slowly do the laxative and supplement it again and repeat the Beej Mantra Kriya in Kumbhak. Do this activity on the Muladhar Chakra for at least 3 minutes, then rise up through the Susumna Nadi and come to the Swadhisthana Chakra, after experiencing the Chakra, connect the Pranavayu to the Chakra.

Apply Kumbhaka on Swadhisthana while feeling the Puraka up to the Chakra. Imagine the scene of "rising sun" with Kumbhaka. During the period of Kumbhaka, mentally chant the seed mantra "Vam" on Swadhisthana. Then do Rechaka and then do Kumbhaka and continue the process. In this way, chant Swadhisthana for 3 minutes.

After completion of chanting at Swadisthan, reach Manipur Chakra through Susumna Nadi. Experience Manipur and connect with life. In this chakra, imagine "desert" and chant "Ram" mantra for 3 minutes. After that, after reaching Anahata Chakra, imagine a "green forest" and chant the seed mantra "Yam" for 3 minutes. After that, after reaching Vishuddhi, chant the Beeja Mantra "Hum" for 3 minutes while imagining "blue sky" on the Chakra.

Then in the same way, reach the Ajna Chakra a little above both the eyebrows through the path of Susumna. Add Pranavayu to Ajna Chakra. Do Kumbhaka after Puraka. At the time of Kumbhak, be free from imagination and watch the scene automatically appearing on the Ajna Chakra. During Kumbhak, mentally chant the seed mantra "Om" on the chakra for 3 minutes. After Ajna Chakra go to Sahasrara Chakra. It is a little difficult to experience Sahasrara, but once it is experienced, it continues to be felt for a long time. Its seed mantra is "Soham". Add vital air to Sahasrara Chakra without doing Kumbhaka. At the time of Puraka, feel that divine energy is going inside through Sahasrara. While inhaling, mentally chant half the seed mantra "So". At the time of rechak, feel that the inner ego is coming out with the breath and along with rechak, mentally chant the remaining half of the mantra "Hum". In this way, after completing the Beej Mantra Kriya till Sahasrar, slowly come out of the "armor".

॥ रेः ॥

CHAPTER SEVEN

Pindastha Meditation

Method-

After reaching Sahasrara by the above method of meditation, when the seeker automatically gets absorbed in Brahmarandhra. After the return state, one returns down from Sahasrara to Mooladhara by passing through each chakra. This process of coming from Muladhara Chakra to Sahasrara and then back from Sahasrara to Muladhara is Pindastha meditation.

॥ णः ॥

CHAPTER EIGHT

Bhavateet Meditation

There are two types of thoughts within oneself, one is thoughts related to enjoyment, the other is thoughts related to feelings. In normal people, thoughts related to enjoyment are voluntary (self-generated and controlled) and in abnormal states, thoughts are involuntary (automatic). When such an adverse event occurs in which thoughts related to enjoyment stop and negative thoughts like sadness, worry, anger, insult come towards the event, then it should be considered as involuntary thoughts related to emotions. The emotional thoughts of an ordinary person often move towards negative situations. In a positive situation, voluntary thoughts related to pleasures become active again.

Through this meditation, in a positive state, thoughts related to emotions are changed from involuntary to voluntary thoughts. This meditation also seems like Pranakarshna meditation, like purification process and energy awakening, but it has been elaborated with different feelings. It can also be said that this meditation is a special form of Pranakarshna meditation.

Method –

Sitting in any meditative posture or lying down in Shavasana. Close your eyes and focus your mind on Pranavayu. First concentrate on Rechak for about 15 minutes and purify your emotions through the following expressions.

Remove the impurity of emotions through laxative.

First of all, remove the ego, then lust, anger, greed, negativity, sorrow, ignorance, enmity, malice, carelessness, misfortune, loss, laziness, thus removing the impurities of all the emotions one by one, then focus on the complementary emotions. Awaken energy.

While supplementing, focus on the divine energies from the universe going inward with the breath, which is giving the power of the following feelings - First, with the supplement, feel the healthy energies going in for 15 minutes, then feel the positive energy going in. Do this, one after the other, inhale the relationship energy, happiness energy, knowledge energy, friendship energy, love energy, protective energy, good luck energy, action energy and finally benefit energy.

After this activity, naturally experience positivity, happiness, joy, love, etc. within and come out of meditation in a normal state by concentrating on breathing again.

Benefit – This meditation awakens emotional power. Awakening the emotional power enriches the life force. This meditation is especially beneficial for unhealthy people, negative people, depression patients, students, those suffering from marital problems and unfortunate people.

Bhav = emotional thoughts

॥ यः ॥

CHAPTER NINE

Susumna Naad Meditation

There is always a sound resonating in this universe. This sound can be heard through Susumna. Some yogis also consider the sound of Susumna Nadi as the sound of Nadyoga or the sound of Omkar.

Method-

Before doing this meditation, the seeker will need a secluded structure where no other sounds can be heard outside or inside and there will be darkness.

You can light it with a lamp for convenience of lighting. Be absolutely right. Before choosing the place of meditation, concentrate the mind inside the brain in any suitable meditative posture or Shavasana. After being completely centered, after a few moments a sound is said from the field of knowledge.

This sound may be of a sestet-like sound, almost like the sound of crickets, or you may hear some other sound. Listen to this sound with concentration for about 20 minutes. After that it should come back to normal state.

Benefits - This meditation awakens the sixth sense and develops self-confidence. Helpful in Kundalini practices.

Susumna Nadi = spinal card

॥ भ: ॥

CHAPTER TEN

Fragrance Meditation (Suvas Meditation)

Suvas means fragrance. Through this meditation, natural aromas reach inside through breathing.

Method –

Keep only one type of fragrant flower like lotus, champa, mogra, kewda. If you have chosen big flowers like lotus, kewda, then keep only 7 flowers, otherwise keep about 35 flowers of small size. Keep the flowers together at the appropriate place and sit in any meditative posture. Fix your mind on breathing for some time. Now if you have big flowers then pick up one flower, otherwise take out 5 small flowers from the left hand and keep them in the right hand. Now take the flower in the right hand and bring it to the nostrils. Again slowly allow the fragrance of the flowers to enter in with a slow complement. Do Kumbhaka for a few moments. Feel that the fragrance is spreading inside. Then do laxative gently.

In this way, do this activity for about 30 minutes and come back to normal state.

Benefits – Happiness increases, very effective on serious diseases.

॥ रूगो : ॥

CHAPTER ELEVEN

Blissful Meditation(Anandmarg Meditation)

Without the attainment of bliss, no yogi can attain the Supreme Being. Through this meditation, the bliss energy flows from the universe and enters the body through a subtle path.

Method-

First of all, lie down in Shavasana, concentrate your mind till the bones. Then imagine that some energy consisting of white light is coming towards you like clouds from the universe. The energy rays from the source of that energy are going towards your feet and entering through the doors of the nails. Feel the movement of this energy moving slowly inside you like an ant.

Experience that this energy gradually spreads through the toenails, inner ankles, knees, thighs, crosses the spine, reaches the hands and head and reaches the entire body. In the end, experiencing the positivity of the energies within, the feet get cut off from the energy flow of the universe and come back to normal state.

Benefit- Anandmarg meditation awakens the subtle energies within. Makes positive.

Shavasna = lie down like a corpse

॥ दे :॥

CHAPTER TWELVE

Shavasana

Not including Shavasana in the category of meditation would be an insult to Shavasana. This is usually done before or after yoga exercises.

Method –

Lie down in Shavasana and close your eyes. Feel the breath reach the lungs. Then feel the entire body moving from the lungs. Feel the negative aspects stuck within the body. Expand consciousness throughout the body. After some time, slowly collect the consciousness with your toes, that is, feel your toes becoming zero. Gradually the emptiness is moving towards the middle part of the body. Gradually the ankles will become void, then moving forward till the knees, further the thighs will become void, through the genitals, after crossing the intestines and navel chakra, the chest will become void.

Emptiness further extends from the shoulders to the elbows and reaches the fingers of the hands. Then Shunyata passes through the neck and voids the face and then Shunyata moves forward and voids the entire head. The whole body becomes void. Only the mind remains. Mind devoid of body and senses. Seeing a dead body coming out of the mind. The mind receives divine energies from outside. The mind becomes powerful and enters the body again. The mind will enter inside and make the body conscious from head to toe. Consciousness started from the encyclopedia of knowledge. Consciousness gradually moves forward, making the eyes and ears conscious, activating the mouth, reaching the chest through the throat, and for a few moments, the consciousness expands there and first passes through the shoulders and elbows and makes the fingers conscious.

Then the consciousness further moves from the chest, through the intestines and navel, through the genitals and crosses the thighs, making the knees conscious and active. Consciousness increases beyond the knees and activates the ankles, making the toes and toes fully conscious. In the end, the whole body comes back to normal state, feeling completely active, alert and excited.

Benefit- This meditation helps in eliminating inner tiredness. It is a sedative for diseases like high blood pressure, heart disease, depression, insomnia. The duration of Shavasana is equal to four times the duration of sleep. That is,

30 minutes of Shavasana done with complete meditation is as beneficial as 2 hours of sleep. If you want to reduce the duration of sleep then do Shavasana daily.

॥ व: ॥

Padastha Meditation

Meditating on the feet of your favorite deity by meditating in your heart from the toenails to the crown is Padastha meditation.

॥ स्य : ॥

Vipassana Meditation

Vipassana is a very ancient method of self-purification through introspection. Vipassana is to see and understand what is exactly as it is. About 2500 years ago, Lord Gautam Buddha re-researched this extinct method and made it widely available as a public cure for public diseases and an art of living. The purpose of this public spiritual practice is to completely eradicate the vices and attain the state of supreme liberation. The purpose of this sadhana is to remove not only physical diseases but also all the sufferings of human beings.

Vipassana is the practice of self-purification through introspection. The practice of Chittavishodhana helps us live a life of happiness and peace by dispassionately observing the changing events taking place in our own body and mind stream from moment to moment. We can experience peace and harmony within ourselves.

The scientific rules according to which our thoughts, disorders, emotions and sensations operate are clear. From our direct experience we know how vices are formed, how bondages are created and how we can get rid of them. We become alert, conscious, controlled and peaceful.

There are three stages of this meditation. First step: The devotees take a vow to observe five precepts, that is, abstaining from violence, theft, lying, celibacy and consumption of intoxicants. By following these principles the mind becomes so calm that it becomes easier to do further work. Next step – practicing a meditation called "Anapan" by concentrating on your natural breathing in and out of the nostrils. By the fourth day, the mind becomes somewhat calm, concentrated and suitable for the practice of Vipassana—being aware of the sensations within your body, understanding their true nature, and maintaining equanimity toward them.

Campers learn the practice of Mangal-Maitri on the tenth day and all living beings are made partners in the virtue acquired during the camp. This sadhana is an exercise of the mind. Just as the body is made healthy through physical exercise, similarly the mind can be made healthy through Vipassana.

Good results come only with continuous practice. It should not be expected that all the problems will be solved within ten days. In ten days, the outline of the sadhana is understood so that the work of implementing Vipassana in life can begin. The more the practice increases, the more one will get relief from suffering and the closer the seeker will move towards the ultimate goal of ultimate liberation. Such good results will definitely come within ten days which will start giving direct benefits in life.

If a yogi tries Vipassana seriously, he acquires an effective technique to attain happiness and peace in life.

॥ धी: ॥

CHAPTER FIFTEEN

Japa Meditation

This is a special meditation taught by spiritual teachers to the disciple at the time of initiation. The benefit of this meditation is obtained after Guru Mantra initiation. Even if you know some mantra, to practice this method it is necessary to get the mantra from a Guru.

Method-

Every chanting mantra has two parts like: Sita-Ram, Radhe-Krishna, Shi-Va, O-M, So-Hum. To chant the mantra with your breath while sitting in any meditation posture, meditate on your Guru, while inhaling, recite the first part of the mantra in your mind and while exhaling, chant the second part of the mantra in your mind.
Benefit: Spiritual awakening.

॥ म : ॥

Preksha Meditation

In present time, Preksha meditation is one of the most popular meditation techniques. It has been formulated by a Jain guru fromIndia, Acharya Mahapragya and is a perfect combination of religion and modern science. Preksha is all about profoundly seeing the self.

Benefits of Preksha meditation-

Preksha meditation helps purification of emotions and consciousness. You can realize the self with Preksha. Its continuous practice brings several positive changes in your personality. With Preksha you can overcome negative emotions and feelings including anger, hatred, jealously, envy, greed, fear, violent behavior, nervousness and emotional disturbance. And at the same time there is enhancement of positivism in your attitude and behavior. It helps increasing will power, memory, self confidence, decision making and understanding. By practicing Preksha there is improvement in psychosomatic diseases. It cleanses and relaxes mind.

At physical level Preksha meditation helps strengthening immunity, controlling blood pressure, improving functioning of nervous system, endocrine system and blood circulation system. With Preksha you can overcome various addictions and bad habit.

Technique of Preksha meditation

Preksha meditation deals with every aspect of human being. It is divided in seven sections. Beginners may practice first three steps.

Kayotsarga (Deep relaxation with self awareness)
Antaryatra (The journey within)
Shwas Preksha (Awareness of breath)
Sharir Preksha (Awareness of body)
Chaitanaya Kendra Preksha (Awareness of psychic centers)

Leshya Dhyan (Awareness of psychic colors)
Anupreksha (Contemplation)

For practicing Preksha meditation you must select a quiet place without disturbance. Spare approximately fifteen minutes in the beginning. This time can be increased gradually to thirty minutes depending on your experience and interest in meditation.

Posture:

Sit either on a chair or on a floor. Keep your body erect with spine straight. In case you are sitting on floor, you can select any of these postures depending on your comfort, lotus posture (padmasana), half lotus posture (ardha padmasana) or simple posture (sukhasana). Your hands must rest on your knees with palms facing upwards. Hands must be in Gyan mudra i.e. index fingers of hands touching thumbs. Gently close your eyes.

In the beginning you can recite any mantra of your choice, likeOmor any other mantra. Chant for nine times.

Meditation:

Kayotsarga (Deep relaxation with self awareness)

Keep your body motionless. Relax various organs of your body. Move your awareness on different parts of your body starting from feet to head and by the process of autosuggestion feel relaxation process on particular parts. Experience every part is relaxed including all muscles, nerves, blood vessels, various organs and systems of your body. And feel your entire body relaxed.

Keep your mind alert and awake during relaxation process.

Duration of this exercise is around ten minutes.

Antaryatra (The journey within)

While maintaining your body in a constant and motionless state, draw your attention on lower end of your spine. This is known as center of energy. Slowly move your attention to upward direction along spinal chord and reach to the top of your head, where brain is located. This end is your center of wisdom. Stay there for few seconds and now move your attention downwards from head to the bottom of spine. Complete cycle from center of energy to center of wisdom and back activates your various hidden powers and facilitates free flow of vital life energy in upward direction.

This process of meditation takes about five minutes.

Shwas Preksha (Awareness of breath)

Breathing is a natural process. You need not pay attention for normal breathing process. Adults normally have a breathing frequency of 12 to 20 breaths per minute. Lowering breathing frequency increases life expectancy. It is said; saints living inIndia go toHimalayas and live for hundreds years as they master their breathing process and reduce their frequency to a great extent.

This meditation helps increasing duration of breaths thus reducing its frequency. This helps increasing chances of longevity and improving efficiency of mental faculties.

With closed eyes take slow but deep breaths. Pay your attention and feel its presence at your naval region. On breathing in, your stomach expands and on breathing out, stomach contracts. Be aware of this expansion and contraction at your naval. Make it sure that not a single breath must go unnoticed. Regulate your inhaling and exhaling process such that it takes equal time. It should be synchronized. Now move your attention to the tip of your nostrils. Create awareness of breathing process. See that you are breathing in and breathing out. While breathing in, feel a sensation of cool air and while exhaling, feel warmth air at the tip of your nostrils. Keep a vigilant eye on movement of breaths.

Later you can add mantra So'ham with breathing process. While breathing in, chant 'So' and on breathing out chant, 'Ham'. Continue this awareness for sometime.

Slowly withdraw your attention from breathing and be aware of your surrounding. Slowly open your eyes. This session of Preksha meditation is over.

This exercise will take ten to fifteen minutes.

With regular practice you can learn to increase the duration of breaths from twelve per minute to eight or six. This helps you keeping healthy and adds year to your life.

Now that you have learnt Preksha meditation, by regular practice you can you can get its benefits.

Wishing you success in all that you do.

॥ हरि: ॥

External Meditation

When the seeker concentrates his mind outside his own body, it is placed in the category of external meditation. There are many methods of external meditation, some of which are as follows.

CHAPTER SEVENTEEN

Nature Listening Meditation

If you want to do something while living in the society, then you must do this meditation. Also, depressed or introverted people get full benefit from this meditation.

Method –

Sitting in a suitable posture amidst nature, closing your eyes and listening to the sounds produced by nature like birds, wind, trees and other creatures. Do not waste time in this meditation, keep doing it as long as you feel happy.

॥ धर्ि: ॥

CHAPTER EIGHTEEN

Nature Meditation

Often man gets trapped in the web of material illusion and becomes far away from nature. This meditation provides a connection with nature and also frees one from worries.

Method-

Go alone to a completely natural place where there is no trace of materialism anywhere. Don't feel alone amidst nature. Create behavior with every object seen in nature with open eyes. Mix with the trees, plants, flowers, animals, water, land, stones etc. There is no contract of time period in this meditation also. As long as you can do it with pleasure, keep doing it.

यो :

CHAPTER NINETEEN

Spiritual Journey Meditation

This meditation refreshes the person doing it with joy and energy. Some of its special methods are –

Method 1-

Sitting in an adapted posture or lying in Shavasana with your eyes closed, take an imaginative journey around your house. Visit social or natural areas around the house. Practice social behavior in meditation. Feel yourself a great man in meditation. You are behaving honestly with people. You are free from lust, anger, pride, greed and arrogance. Feel your face happy. Call yourself Buddha, Jesus. One can mingle in the society even after considering himself as Krishna. Later, after reaching the place of meditation, he came back to normal state.

Method 2-

Sitting in an adapted posture, close your eyes and feel your vital consciousness, feel that you have been subtly lifted into the air. Slowly rising up, you are traveling in space. Consider yourself the center of the universe. Realize that first, you are attracting divine energies from all around the universe. After attracting the energies for some time, you are providing energy to the biosphere. After some time, gradually become comfortable.

॥ यो ॥

Chitti Vritti Nirodh Meditation

This meditation is effective in stabilizing and calming the mind in a few moments.

Method –

Lie down in Shavasana and feel yourself lying on the water on the seashore. The lower half of the body should feel like wet water and the upper half of the body should be open towards the sky. Your part is in water, feel the waves of water on that part. Feel the waves rolling violently. Feel the waves gradually calming down. Slowly feel the mind becoming calm as the waves calm down. After some time, the waves will become completely stable, with which the mind will also be able to feel completely calm and stable. Experience a calm mind for some time and come to a comfortable state.

॥ न: ॥

CHAPTER TWENTY-ONE

Death Sensation Meditation (Marnabhuti Meditation)

This meditation is suitable for those who have a strong fear of death. Respected Gurudev said that by practicing this meditation, the seeker can attain salvation at the time of actual death.

Method-

Sit in a suitable asana or Shavasana and close your eyes and experience yourself in the final state of death. Experience the pain at the time of Prana leaving the body and feel the separation of Prana from the body. After that, remain quiet for a few moments and then become comfortable.

॥ पूर ॥

CHAPTER TWENTY-TWO

Hellish Meditation (Narkanubhuti Meditation)

Hellish meditation is not an ordinary meditation but a mystery. I had heard about this meditation that through this, the evil deeds of previous births can be eliminated by suffering the consequences. If anyone has committed any grave sin in his previous birth, then he will have to bear the consequences of it in the same way as when Ram killed Bali secretly, then in the next life, Bali disguised himself as a maid and shot an arrow at Ram in the form of Krishna.

Method-

Lying in Shavasana or sitting in a meditative posture and closing your eyes, first meditate on the feeling of death and then experience your soul being taken away by the messengers of Yama. Imagine the terrible gates of hell. Enter the door. See all the scenes of torture inside.

Somewhere people were being thrown into hot cauldrons of oil, somewhere they were being whipped, somewhere they were being thrown into snake pits, somewhere they were being burnt by pouring oil, somewhere they were being scratched by birds and animals and somewhere they were being skinned alive. You have to be ready to endure these tortures. First you were physically created, then Yamdoot caught you and put you in a boiling cauldron of oil. Feel the pain of being boiled in a boiling pan and then feel yourself burning to death in the same pan. Again you have been given a new body, be ready to face the next torture. You are being beaten with sharp whips. Feel the hurt and pain of the whips. Yamdoot whipped you to death, feel death again. Similarly, experience death again and again through different types of tortures one after the other. Then for some time, experience natural peace and joy and come back to the physical state.

॥ चो ॥

CHAPTER TWENTY-THREE

Divine Realization Meditation(Parmatmanubhuti)

Through this meditation, the real experience of God is achieved, the path of Yoga does not consider the form of God in any particular object but considers the entire world as the form of God.

Method -

Stand alone in the lap of nature and feel God in every particle from nature to infinity. Believe that God is always watching you and experience God's presence.

God = Pramatma

॥ ६ ॥

CHAPTER TWENTY-FOUR

External Trataka Meditation

External Tratak is considered to be an important tool for increasing concentration. Tantrikas also have to practice Tratak to achieve success in their Tantra practice.

Method -

Choose such a place for Tratak where there is neither much nor less light. You should place the image of the above point at a place from where the point falls exactly when you sit.

In the morning, when there is neither less nor more light, sit at a selected place and measure a distance of 1 hand from the point with your eyes. Do some eye exercises. Then start staring at the dot without blinking. Try to watch continuously for 5 minutes. After completing the exercise, close your eyes for some time and allow yourself to calm down. Gradually, as you practice, you can increase the time interval over a few days.

Benefits - This meditation increases concentration and eye power.

॥ यात् ॥

Meditation Teacher Training Course

Certificate Course

Duration : 150 Hours

Board : International Yoga Organization (Miistry of Ayush & United Nation Registerd)

Study Centre : Jag Kalyan Organization , Rishi Kuteer, Prithviganj, Pratapgarh, Uttar Pradesh, India 230304

Study Plateform : Online (You can read this book and give the online examination by paying the course fee. If you fail in the exam, you can apply for re-examination free of cost.)

Contact : 8306907788 (English Mrdium)

Fee : ?10000 INR

Transaction QR Code

After Payment send Screenshot to +91-7984261748 (WhatsApp), Your Details & Program Name

Other Courses : Diploma Program in Yoga(DPY), Chakras Analysis & Balancing, Ayurveda & Yoga Awarness Program, Yoga Teacher Traning 200 hr & 500 hr

Author Book List

Sr.No.	Book Name	Price (Inr)
1	Jyotish Rahsya Part 01(Hindi)	165
2	Sushma Puran (Hindi)	155
3	Ajna Tarot Cards ((Hindi & English)	243
4	Kalaunji Rahasya (Hindi)	100
5	Hanuman Chalisa (Hindi)	10
6	Prakritik Chikitsa Darshan (Gujrati)	99
7	Secret Door For Success (English)	99
8	N.D.D.Y. First Year Second Paper (Eng. & Hindi)	235
9	Basic Naturopathy And Ayurveda (English)	205
10	N.D.D.Y. 1ST YEAR 1ST PAPER (Hindi)	190
11	Life Experience Of Naturopathy Lovers (Hindi)	99
12	A Planet Of Red Mountain (English)	240
13	A Planet Of Red Mountain (Hindi)	99
14	Kalki –Part 1 (Hindi)	150
15	The Prosperity From The Mating (English)	150
16	Gandhi –A Successful Ashtanga Yogi(Hindi)	105
17	The Secret Of 7 Chakras And Kundalini (English)	910
17	The Secret Of 7 Chakras & Activation Of Chakras (Hindi)	540
18	Manas Bhajan Sangrah(Hindi)	150
19	The Secret Of Soul (Hindi)	115
20	Dhyan Rahsya (Hindi)	450
21	Common Acute And Chronic Disease To Cure By Naturopathy (English)	260
22	The Glory Of Shriram (English)	150
23	Jyotish Rahasya Part 1	165

Avilable on Flipcart, Amazon & notionpress.com